YOUR
STRONG
SKELETON
and ↙
AMAZING
Muscular System

FIND OUT HOW YOUR BODY WORKS!

Paul Mason

Crabtree Publishing Company
www.crabtreebooks.com

Crabtree Publishing Company

www.crabtreebooks.com

1-800-387-7650

Published in Canada
Crabtree Publishing
616 Welland Avenue
St. Catharines, ON
L2M 5V6

Published in the United States
Crabtree Publishing
PMB 59051
350 Fifth Ave, 59th Floor
New York, NY 10118

Author: Paul Mason
Editorial director: Kathy Middleton
Editors: Annabel Stones, Shirley Duke, Kelly Spence
Designer: Rocket Design (East Anglia) Ltd
Consultant: John Clancy, Former Senior
   Lecturer in Applied Human Physiology
Proofreaders: Susie Brooks, Rebecca Sjonger
Prepress technician: Margaret Amy Salter
Print and production coordinator: Margaret Amy Salter

Published by Crabtree Publishing Company in 2016

First published in 2015 by Wayland
Copyright © Wayland, 2015

Picture credits:
Getty Images: p11 cr Stephen Oliver, p19 tr Keystone / Stringer, p22 br Sciepro, p25 bl DEA / G DAGLI ORTI, p29 br Ian Cook / Contributor; Science Photo Library: p15 br SOVEREIGN, ISM, p20 TED KINSMAN; Shutterstock: Cover, p3 b, p5 cl, p5 cr, p5 br, p6, p7 c, p7 r, p7 bl, p8 l, p8 r, p9 t, p9 b, p10, p11 l, p12, p13 r, p14 tl, p14 b, p17 br, p18 tl, p18 br, p19 cl, p19 br, p21 tr, p21 bl, p21 br, p23 all, p24, p25 br, p26 Natursports, p27 tl, p27 br, p28 bl, p28 br, p29 tr, p29 cl.
Graphic elements from Shutterstock.

Artwork: Stefan Chabluk: p3 t, p3 cr, p4, p13 l, p15 t, p17 c, p25 t; Ian Thompson: p3 cl, p16, p22 l, p27 cl.

Every effort has been made to clear copyright. Should there be any inadvertent omission, please apply to the publisher for rectification.

The website addresses (URLs) included in this book were valid at the time of going to press. However, it is possible that contents or addresses may have changed since the publication of this book. No responsibility for any such changes can be accepted by either the author or the Publisher.

Printed in the USA/082015/SN20150529

Library and Archives Canada Cataloguing in Publication

Mason, Paul, 1967-, author
   Your strong skeleton and amazing muscular system / Paul Mason.

(Your brilliant body!)
Includes index.
Issued in print and electronic formats.
ISBN 978-0-7787-2208-3 (bound).--ISBN 978-0-7787-2226-7 (paperback).--
ISBN 978-1-4271-1711-3 (pdf).--ISBN 978-1-4271-1705-2 (html)

   1. Musculoskeletal system--Juvenile literature. 2. Bones--Juvenile literature. 3. Muscles--Juvenile literature. I. Title.

QM100.M37 2015   j612.7   C2015-903177-X
                               C2015-903178-8

Library of Congress Cataloging-in-Publication Data

Mason, Paul, 1967-
   Your strong skeleton and amazing muscular system / Paul Mason.
      pages cm. -- (Your brilliant body!)
   Includes index.
   ISBN 978-0-7787-2208-3 (reinforced library binding : alk. paper) --
   ISBN 978-0-7787-2226-7 (pbk. : alk. paper) --
   ISBN 978-1-4271-1711-3 (electronic pdf : alk. paper) --
   ISBN 978-1-4271-1705-2 (electronic html : alk. paper)
   1. Human skeleton--Juvenile literature. 2. Musculoskeletal system--Juvenile literature. I. Title.

QM101.M327 2016
611--dc23
                         2015015365

CONTENTS

Cells are the building blocks of life. These are skeletal muscle cells.

muscle cell

muscle tissue

Muscle cells join together in long strands called fibers. The fibers join together to form muscle tissue.

Muscle tissue can form muscles (organs), such as those in your arms and legs.

Your muscles work together to form your musculoskeletal system. This includes your bones and muscles—organs that help you move around.

YOUR AMAZING BONES AND MUSCLES

BRILLIANT BODY FACT

The hyoid bone in your throat is the only bone that doesn't connect with any other bone.

What's the reason you aren't blobbing around on the floor like a jellyfish right now? Your BONES! They provide a structure for your body—like a snail's shell, or a suit of armor, but on the inside. Your bones and muscles give your body its shape.

Joining together

As a baby you had over 300 bones—but as you grew, some of them **fused** together. For example, your skull starts off as eight soft, bony plates with gaps between them. There are good things and bad things about this arrangement:

Good things: It allows a baby's skull to compress in the narrow birth canal; after you're born, it also lets your skull expand as your brain grows.

Bad things: A **flexible** skull doesn't provide very much brain protection.

LOOK CLOSER
SKULL PLATES

infant skull

spaces between bone plates

adult skull

Soon after you were born, the bones in your skull started to join together. By the time you were about 18 months old, your skull had become a strong helmet (under your skin). As you grow, bones fuse in some other parts of the body, too. By the time you reach adulthood, your 300+ bones have become just 206.

Muscle magic

Of course, bones alone can't do much. To stand up straight, sit, and lie down, you also need muscles. These work like tug-of-war teams, pulling your bones back and forth as instructed by your brain.

DID YOU KNOW?
Without bones, you couldn't speak.

Humans have a little bone called a hyoid in their throats. It works with the voice box and tongue, and makes speech possible. The hyoid bone acts as an anchor for the tongue, attaching it to the throat at one end. This gives the tongue a wide range of movement.

hyoid bone

The jaw muscle is very strong. You use it for everything from laughing to eating.

See for yourself

Test your muscle movement!

Hold your arm out straight with your palm up. Put your other hand on top, between the elbow and shoulder. It's now resting on your biceps muscle.

Next bend your arm, so that your fingertips touch your shoulder. The biceps muscle went from long to bunched-up, as it pulled your arm into a bent shape.

Bones are connected by joints. Muscles pull the bones on either side of the joints—which is what makes activities such as running possible.

AN ENGINEERING MIRACLE

If your bones were made entirely of what most people THINK of as bone (the hard outer shell), it would be almost impossible to walk. Your legs would be so heavy that your muscles wouldn't be strong enough to move them!

BRILLIANT BODY FACT

Your smallest bone is deep in your ear, and is the size of a grain of rice.

LOOK CLOSER

INSIDE A BONE

This diagram shows a long bone—one that is longer than it is wide.

medullary cavity
A long, hollow cavity containing bone marrow.

shaft
The long part of a bone.

bone marrow

cartilage
A cushion of soft tissue.

blood vessels
These deliver nutrients, and collect waste and new blood cells.

compact bone
The bone's hard outer shell.

spongy bone
This is lighter than compact bone.

head

Light and strong

Bones contain some smart engineering that makes them lighter than you might expect. Only the outer parts are made of hard, heavy compact bone. The inner parts are lighter as they are made of **spongy bone**—a web of thin pieces of bone with spaces between them.

Inside your bones

The hollow cavity inside your bones is filled with **bone marrow**. This spongy, flexible substance is very important. In infants all bone marrow is red and produces red blood cells. In adults, only some bone marrow is red. Most is yellow and serves as storage for body fat.

Bone types

Bones are named according to their shape. Those with a long middle section are called **long bones**. You also have four other types:

* **Flat bones** have wide, flat surfaces, like the ones that make up your skull and hips.

* **Short bones** are roughly as wide as they are long.

* **Sesamoid bones** are flat bones, such as your kneecap, that are held in place by a **tendon** (the end of a muscle).

* **Irregular bones** are oddly shaped bones that do not fit into any other category, such as the **vertebrae** in your back, or the mandible (lower jaw).

STRANGE BUT TRUE!

The largest bone in your body is your **pelvis**—though it's actually made of six bones that joined firmly together as you grew. Your longest bone is the **femur** in the thigh. It stretches for almost 25% of your total height.

pelvis

femur

This close-up view shows the hollow spaces inside spongy bone.

DID YOU KNOW?

Bone is stronger than some kinds of steel.

The outer layer of your bones—the layer known as compact bone—is REALLY tough. In fact, it's so tough that if you made an exact replica of a bone with an outer layer of steel, instead of compact bone, it wouldn't be as strong!

THE STAGGERING SPINE

That's staggering as in "amazing," not staggering as in "walking around looking as though you're about to fall down." In fact, it's your spine that STOPS you from falling down. This amazing collection of bones is the most important in your body.

Protect and support

Your spine has two very important jobs. First, it protects the **spinal cord**—a thick bundle of nerves that carries messages between the brain and the rest of your body. Without this, you cannot walk, kick a ball, swim, or do anything physical. Second, your spine supports your upper body, from your bottom to the base of your skull. To do these two jobs it has to be both strong and flexible.

Your spine is incredibly flexible.

See for yourself

Find your spine!

Feel around behind you. Touch your backbone. You should be able to feel a series of little bony knobs. Each one is part of a vertebra.

You're not feeling the main part of the vertebrae. Each has three little **spurs** sticking out—two to the sides and one to the back. What you're feeling is the backward-pointing spur.

What's a spine made of?

A full-grown spine is made of a stack of 26 bones, called vertebrae. (A single one is called a vertebra.) Each vertebra has a hole in it for the spinal cord to pass through. The vertebrae are separated by soft pads called discs.

Your spine is connected to over 100 different muscles, which allow it to bend in almost any direction. This structure allows the spine to be flexible, and protects the spinal cord.

LOOK CLOSER
THE SPINE

The spine is divided into five areas.

cervical spine (vertebrae C1–C7)

thoracic spine (vertebrae T1–T12)

lumbar spine (vertebrae L1–L5)

sacrum (fused vertebrae S1–S5)

coccyx (fused vertebrae C1–C4 also called the tailbone)

STRANGE BUT TRUE!

When a baby is born it has 33 vertebrae in its spine. As it grows, some of them fuse together. A fully grown adult has 26 vertebrae in his or her spine.

DID YOU KNOW?

You're taller in the morning.

Together, the discs between your vertebrae make up over 25% of your spine's length. When you're upright, the discs are squashed down. They expand again when you lie down. The effect is that you are just a little shorter at the end of the day than at the beginning.

Almost unbelievably, a giraffe's neck has the same number of bones as a human's. The giraffe's are a bit longer, though.

Some of a giraffe's neck vertebrae can be up to ten inches (25 cm) long!

BODY ARMOR

Most people, at some time, fall off a bike, tumble out of a tree, get run into while playing sports, or bang their head on a low doorway. So it's a good thing that your bones don't only work as a framework for your body. Some also work like a suit of armor, protecting **vital** organs from damage.

An adult's skull is a fused dome of bone.

Your body's helmet

Your skull protects your most important organ—your brain. It works a bit like a helmet under your skin, stopping anything from making contact with your brain and damaging it.

Of course, your skull has to be light enough for you to be able to move your head, so it can't be TOO thick. This is why it's a good idea to give it some backup, by wearing an actual helmet for activities such as cycling, horseback riding, and skateboarding.

A protective cage

Your ribs form a layer of protection for important organs such as your heart and lungs, protecting them from damage. They wrap right around your upper body, protecting the front, sides, and back.

Together, your ribs, **sternum**, and the top of your spine are called the **rib cage**. The top seven pairs are known as the **true ribs** and attach to the spine and to the sternum.

The next three pairs attach to the spine and to each other—they are called **false ribs**. At the bottom are the **floating ribs**, which are only attached to your spine.

Rib bones are very **fragile**. (You can damage a rib with a violent sneeze!) They act like a car's crumple zone, breaking to absorb the force of a blow. Your ribs are joined together by muscles, which means that the rib cage is flexible and can expand when you breathe in.

PHRENOLOGY
BY
L.N.FOWLER.

Phrenology was a kind of "pretend" science that was popular in the nineteenth century. Phrenologists believed that the size and shape of the skull was linked to a person's character.

LOOK CLOSER
THE RIBCAGE

True ribs attach to the sternum—a long, flat plate of bone at the front of your chest.

true ribs

sternum

false ribs

floating ribs

DID YOU KNOW?

Celebrities DON'T have ribs removed to make them look thin.

This is an old urban myth—that some celebrities have had their lowest ribs removed, to give them a slimmer waistline. The same myth was once circulated about Victorian ladies who wore very tight corsets to follow the fashion of the time.

BEND, DON'T BREAK

If you bend a bone, it breaks. But humans, who are built of bone, have to bend all the time. Just think how tricky a forward roll or a cartwheel would be with a spine made of one long bone, instead of 26 smaller, connected ones!

The skeleton

Your skeleton is made up of more than 200 separate bones. These all have to be connected, otherwise you would simply be a big heap of bones. The place where two or more bones meet is called a joint. To stop bones from slipping and sliding apart, you have **ligaments**. These hold your bones in place in the joint.

Moveable joints

Some joints cannot move at all, such as those between the bony plates in your skull. Other joints allow a small amount of movement, like those between the bones in your spine (see pages 8–9). Many joints move freely, such as the ones in your wrist or ankle.

Types of joint

Your body has three main types of joint, named according to what they are made of.

✳ **Fibrous joints** are inflexible and hold together bones such as your skull plates, and the two bones in your forearm.

DID YOU KNOW?

Snake oil doesn't work!

In the 1800s, joint-pain medicines were known as "snake oil." They were said to make you as flexible as a snake. Salesmen even hired **contortionists** to show how effective their snake oil was!

Sadly, the medicines did not work.

* **Cartilaginous joints** bind bones together in a more flexible way than fibrous joints. For example, cartilaginous joints connect your ribs. That's why your rib cage can expand when you breathe in.

* **Synovial joints** are the most common kind of joint. Here, a fluid-filled sac separates two bones. The bones are often connected by ligaments—tough strands of fiber that hold the joint in position.

DON'T TRY THIS AT HOME!

Major Zamora was a well-known contortionist in the United States during the early 1900s. Zamora was only 2'8" (81 cm) tall, and weighed just 53 pounds (24 kg), but he was also incredibly flexible. He could get through tiny holes—his most famous trick was squeezing himself into a large bottle, then climbing out again.

LOOK CLOSER
SYNOVIAL JOINT

cartilage pad at end of bone

ligament

synovial sac

bone

synovial fluid

tendon

A synovial joint is the most common type in the human body.

Contortionists, like the two girls here, have often trained since they were small children.

BONES FOR TRICKY JOBS

Think about your arm. It has a simple job—all it has to do is bend at the elbow. So the bones in your arm are simple: just one main bone in your upper arm and two in your lower arm. Now think about the hundreds of jobs your hands and feet do. No wonder they contain a lot of bones!

Hands and feet

Your hands and feet are used for delicate jobs such as playing the guitar, dancing, petting the cat, and so on. Imagine trying to play the guitar if your fingers only contained one long, straight bone—it would be impossible! Fortunately, each of your hands contains 27 bones, and each foot has just one fewer—26.

LOOK CLOSER
FOOT BONES

midfoot
bones that arch the middle of the foot

hindfoot
heel and ankle bones

forefoot
five toes, plus five longer bones called **metatarsals**

Muscle-free hands

Bones are moved by muscles, which are usually located nearby. If your fingers contained muscles, though, each one would be as big as a sausage. So, amazingly, there are NO muscles in your fingers. Instead, the tendons in your fingers are connected to muscles in the palms of your hands and your forearm.

Multi-purpose feet

Your feet allow you to balance, which is essential for all sorts of actions—simply walking or running, as well for dancing, gymnastics, or pedaling your bike. As a result, feet are almost as complicated as hands. They have just one bone fewer per foot—plus 33 joints, 107 ligaments, and 19 muscles.

LOOK CLOSER
TENDONS IN THE HAND

Small muscles allow fine movement.

Tendons stretching from the inside forearm muscles bend the lower part of the fingers.

Tendons from muscles in the outside forearm allow the hand to open up.

See for yourself

Some fingers share tendons with their next door neighbors. Try this experiment as a demonstration:

Hold your hand out with the palm facing you. Now bend your little finger. Is it the only one that moves? Do the same experiment with your other fingers and your thumb. Can you move any fingers without one of the others moving too?

STRANGE BUT TRUE!

As this X-ray shows, not everyone is born with ten fingers and ten toes. Having more than the usual number is called **polydactylism**.

MARVELOUS MUSCLES

BRILLIANT BODY FACT

When you walk, you use about 200 different muscles!

If you didn't have muscles, you couldn't turn a page of this book. You also couldn't eat, breathe, sneeze, flick your older brother's ear, or run away. In fact, you couldn't make ANY of the millions of movements you make every day. Without muscles, you would literally be going nowhere!

other muscle stays relaxed. Then, to move the joint in the other direction, the muscles change jobs. The first muscle relaxes, while the second one shortens itself and pulls.

Types of muscle

The muscles you use to move around are called **skeletal muscles**. Your body also comes equipped with two other types—**smooth muscle** and **cardiac muscle**. You can find out more about these on page 21.

Working in pairs

Most skeletal muscles are attached to bones on either side of a joint (see pages 12 and 13). Each joint has a pair of muscles. While one muscle in the pair shortens itself (**contracts**) and pulls, the

LOOK CLOSER
MOVING MUSCLES

When one muscle is contracting (pulling), the opposite muscle is relaxed.

The biceps muscle contracts and shortens to bend the arm.

The triceps muscle is relaxed and long.

The biceps muscle lengthens as it relaxes.

The triceps muscle contracts slightly to straighten the arm.

What is a muscle made of?

Skeletal muscles are made of long tubes called **fascicles**. Inside each fascicle are long muscle fibers. These are separated into slow-twitch and fast-twitch fibers, depending on how quickly they can contract. Fast-twitch muscle fibers are used for short bursts of activity, such as a sprint, while slow-twitch are used for longer, slower activity, such as walking.

✳ **Fast-twitch** muscle fibers contract very quickly. They do not need oxygen, but they run out of energy very quickly.

✳ **Slow-twitch** muscle fibers do not contract quickly, but keep working for a long time. They make energy using oxygen and food obtained from your blood.

LOOK CLOSER
INSIDE A MUSCLE

muscle fiber made of muscle cells

fascicle

muscle

bone

tendon

DID YOU KNOW?

Your biggest muscle is behind you.

It is in your bottom and is called the **gluteus maximus**. It helps to move your hips and thighs when you walk.

See for yourself

Next time you eat chicken, have a look at the different colors of the meat.

✳ The dark leg meat is slow-twitch muscle, used for low-energy walking around. Its dark color comes from the blood supply needed by slow-twitch muscles.

✳ White breast meat is mostly fast-twitch muscle, designed to power the wings in high-energy bursts. It does not need oxygen for energy, and contains fewer blood vessels.

MUSCLE POWER

Each year a competition is held to decide the "World's Strongest Man." Contestants compete in events from lifting concrete balls to pulling amazingly heavy trucks. But how do they make their muscles so strong?

How do muscles grow?

Muscles grow larger by being used. When you use a muscle, it damages the muscle fibers. Harder use results in more damage. When the body repairs the damaged muscles, it makes them larger. It's the body's way of preparing the muscles, in case they are asked to produce more power again.

Amazing muscles

We all develop our muscle power and size as we grow. The more you use your muscles, the more toned and strong they will become. This means that everyday tasks are easier and also that you develop **endurance**—the ability to keep going longer before you tire. For muscles to become even stronger, they need to be used even more.

Powerful muscles

The most powerful muscle in your body is your jaw muscle. The tongue would be a contender—but it actually contains eight muscles, so it is disqualified. Your most over-powered muscles are the muscles of your eye. These are about 100 times stronger than they really need to be for moving a lightweight eyeball around.

Six pairs of muscles work together to move the eyes in almost any direction.

Cramp!

Sometimes, your muscles suddenly tighten up, without you asking them to. It can be very painful! We call this painful tightening cramps. It usually happens while people are exercising, but you can also get a cramp after exercise, especially if your muscles have been working hard. The best way to get rid of it is by gently stretching the muscle out, and rubbing it to help it relax.

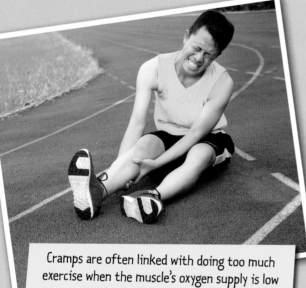

Cramps are often linked with doing too much exercise when the muscle's oxygen supply is low or with not drinking enough fluid.

STRANGE BUT TRUE!

In 1957, an American weight lifter called Paul Anderson decided to show just how powerful his muscles were. He loaded up a table with car parts and a safe full of lead—then lifted it up! It seems to have weighed 6,270 pounds (2,844 kg)*—the greatest weight ever lifted by a human, before or since.

*That's nearly three medium-sized great white sharks!

DID YOU KNOW?

You can't grow new muscles.

Humans are born with all the muscle fibers they will ever have, so you cannot grow new muscle fibers. What CAN happen is that each fiber in a muscle can grow thicker and longer. This happens when the muscles are used—which is why working out at the gym makes your muscles larger.

MUSCLES OUT OF CONTROL!

Have you ever stayed in cold water for too long, or ignored your mom when she told you to put on a coat before going out? If so, you have probably ended up with your teeth chattering and your whole body shaking. Which proves you can't always control your muscles—sometimes, your body just takes over.

What makes you shiver?

Shivering is a **reflex**—something your body does automatically in response to a situation. In this case, it's a response to getting cold. Your body knows that when you use muscles, they warm up and give off heat.

So the **central nervous system** sends an automatic signal to muscles all over your body, telling them to contract many times really quickly.

Other common reflex actions

Shivering is just one of the muscle movements we don't control. Other reflex actions include:

* **ducking** if something is thrown toward your head;

* **quickly lifting your foot** if you step on something sharp;

* **jerking back** if you accidentally touch something hot.

In this image, red = hot, blue = cold. You can see how much heat the weight-lifter's arms are releasing!

These are all examples of your central nervous system taking control of your skeletal muscles. Normally you control these yourself. But in an emergency, your nervous system steps in.

Smooth and cardiac muscles

As well as skeletal muscles, you have smooth and cardiac (heart) muscles. Smooth muscle makes up many of your internal organs, such as your lungs and stomach. These are muscles you NEVER have to think about controlling. Imagine having to remind your heart to beat, your stomach to process food, or your lungs to breathe all the time!

LOOK CLOSER
SMOOTH MUSCLE

smooth muscle cells

Many organs in the digestive system are made of smooth muscle.

Muscles contract and relax to move food through the stomach.

STRANGE BUT TRUE!

Babies are born with "primitive reflexes," which disappear as they grow. One of these is the grasp reflex. Touching a baby's hand will cause it to curl around in a tight grasp. This reflex disappears when a baby is four to six months old.

The cells of heart muscle are Y-shaped. Each tip links to another cell, making the network of cells very strong.

DID YOU KNOW?

One muscle never stops working.

Your heart is the hardest-working muscle in your body. It never stops. When you are resting, a healthy heart beats between 50 and 90 times per minute on average. Usually a child's heart beats faster than an adult's.

FACING FACTS

You have more than 40 muscles in your face. Without them, life would be very dull—you could not eat, speak, or show your feelings. Just try looking surprised, or angry, without moving any part of your face!

Emotional muscles

How can you tell what someone else is feeling? By looking at his or her face! Your face contains the most complex set of muscles in your body, and allows you to show your emotions. Frowning, laughing, crying, looking down your nose at people—these are all messages about how you're feeling. We make most of these emotional muscle movements automatically, without thinking about them.

Practical muscles

Of course, the muscles in your face have practical jobs to do. They allow you to chew your food, sniff the air, talk, drink, blink, and look around. This is why the **temporomandibular joint** (the one that joins your jaw to your skull) is one of the most complicated in the body. It has to be able to move in all directions.

temporomandibular joint

The main facial muscles can be grouped into eye muscles, nose muscles, and mouth muscles.

DID YOU KNOW?

It is possible to guess when someone is lying.

Trained observers can use the automatic muscle movements of our faces to guess when someone is lying.

Here are our top four clues that someone may not be being absolutely honest:

(1) **False facial expressions are usually asymmetrical.**

So, for example, if someone smiles with only one side of their face, they probably aren't really happy.

(2) **It is almost impossible to control the muscles around your eyes.**

It is easy to make your mouth into a smiling shape—but tricky to make your eyes crinkle up convincingly, unless you REALLY feel happy or amused.

(3) **Most people hide other emotions behind a smile.**

If you spot someone giving you a false smile, it's usually because they are trying to hide a different emotion. Ask yourself what it might be!

(4) **Sad chins reveal a faker.**

Nine out of ten people find it impossible to deliberately lower the corners of their mouth and look sad without using their chin muscles. People who are REALLY sad don't do this. So if you see the chin muscles move, the "sad" person is probably faking it.

See for yourself

Read the "Did you know?" panel then test the clues on a friend. Eventually, with practice, they might be able to fake it convincingly.

If this happens, remember—someone who has gotten away with being dishonest will NOT be able to stop a split-second look of triumph.

23

BREAKING BONES

Your body has ways of healing itself and repairing almost any body part that gets broken or damaged. In fact, some of the only body parts that cannot be fixed are your teeth. If you break or damage your adult teeth, there is nothing your body can do (but a dentist CAN fix them).

Keeping straight

Some breaks cause the bones to go out of line. To heal properly, they need to be kept straight. Doctors take an X-ray to see what position the bones are in so that they can then move them into a straight position. To keep them straight, and to stop them moving, you normally have to wear a **plaster cast** until the break has healed.

How do bones mend?

When you break a bone your body is quick to respond. First, it produces lots of new cells and blood vessels at the site of the break. The new cells build up on the broken bone, like a bridge being built over a riverbank. Eventually, they meet new cells that have been growing from the other side of the break, and the bone is healed.

Fractured, or splintered, bones usually heal in one to two months, though it depends on how serious the fracture was.

DID YOU KNOW?

Some saws won't cut.

When you break a bone, you often have to wear a plaster cast. Later, the plaster cast is cut off with a whirring saw. The funny thing is, the worst the saw can do is tickle you!

This is because the saw works by vibrating against the hard cast. Once it touches skin, the skin (which isn't hard) just vibrates up and down with the saw. It tickles, but it doesn't cut.

LOOK CLOSER
MENDING BONES

Broken bones can heal themselves. How long it takes will depend on how bad the break is.

swelling

fibers and cartilage

woven bone

blood vessels

1. Broken blood vessels form a swelling.

2. New cells form a soft tissue between the bone pieces.

3. The soft tissue becomes harder and bone-like.

4. A strong bone patch forms over the break.

DON'T TRY THIS AT HOME!

Sandals were the footwear of choice in ancient Egypt, but these were EXTREMELY difficult to walk in if you had lost your big toe.

Fortunately, the ancient Egyptians developed the world's first functional **prosthetic** bone. It was an artificial big toe, and was designed to make it possible to wear sandals if you had lost your big toe in an accident.

STRANGE BUT TRUE!

Arms are among the bones adults break most often, making up almost half of the total number. Among children, the collarbone is the most commonly broken bone.

TEARS AND STRAINS

Have you ever watched track athletics, soccer, or any other sport where people run fast? If so, you have probably seen someone suddenly *stop* running fast and clutch the back of their leg. The commentator might say something like, "Looks like a torn muscle." So, just what is a torn muscle?

Injury time

A torn muscle is a muscle that has been pulled apart, partly or completely. Other common injuries include damaging the tendons at the ends of a muscle, or the ligaments of a joint. Usually the body can heal itself or adapt, but for serious injuries an operation may be needed to repair the damage.

Torn muscles

Muscles get torn for many reasons. The most common are doing sudden, hard activity, such as picking up a heavy weight, without warming up (see page 29). Muscles also sometimes tear because they have been stretched too far, for example when one of your feet skids and you do the splits.

Snapping tendons

Tendons join muscles to bones. In younger people, tendons are very strong. Their muscles usually tear before one of the tendons breaks. As people get older, though, their tendons weaken. It becomes more likely that their tendon will break, rather than the muscle tearing.

Players warm up before a game and cool down afterward to prevent injuries.

26

STRANGE BUT TRUE!

The **palmaris longus** is the tendon crabs use to open and close their claws. Unless you have claws, you don't really need one.

LOOK CLOSER
TOUGH TENDONS

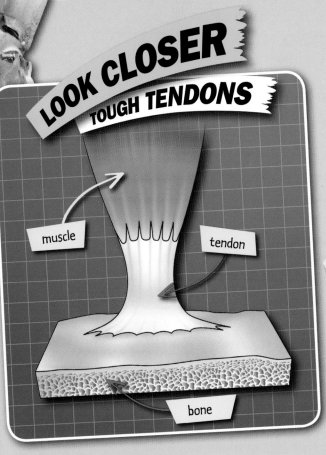

muscle

tendon

bone

Tearing ligaments

Ligaments are strips of tough fiber that hold joints in place. If the joint is forced out of position, like when you step on something and twist your ankle, the ligaments can be damaged or torn completely. The joints most often affected by ligament damage are the knees and ankles.

See for yourself

Your wrist might contain a tendon called the palmaris longus...

Only about 14% of people do not have this tendon. To check if you do:

① Touch the tips of your little finger and thumb together

② Bend your wrist towards you.

If you have a palmaris longus, you will be able to see the tendon clearly, sticking up along the center of your wrist.

DON'T TRY THIS AT HOME!

An ancient Greek myth tells the story of Achilles's heel. Achilles's mom was told that he would one day be killed in battle. She didn't like this idea, so she dunked him into a magical river. This made his body like armor—apart from his heel, which she had held onto. Years later, Achilles was busy attacking the city of Troy when a poisoned arrow hit his heel. Achilles died. Today, the tendon in your heel is named the Achilles tendon in his memory.

MAINTENANCE AND SERVICING

Your bones are continuously being broken down and replaced. After about seven years, none of the original bone is left—you have a new one! However, after the age of about 30, your bone production slows down. More bone is broken down than is made, which is why fractures are more common among the elderly.

Boosting your bones

Fortunately, there is some good news. By building strong bones when you are young, you can can delay your bones' disappearing act. So, how do you go about it?

① Think (and drink) calcium

Calcium is an important mineral for building bone. It also helps your muscles to function and keeps your heart beating efficiently. Your body gets calcium from milk and cheese,

green-leaf vegetables, soya beans, nuts, and fish such as sardines.

② Back up the vitamin D

Your body uses vitamin D to turn calcium into bone. You can eat it in shrimp, sardines (again), egg yolks, or tuna fish. Or you can just get 15 minutes of sunshine every other day—which stimulates your body to produce vitamin D.

Your body can get calcium from milk.

Sunlight helps you produce vitamin D.

③ Exercise

Bones (and muscles) get stronger if they need to get stronger. If you sit around playing video games all day, your body doesn't waste energy making your bones strong. If you go out for a run, skateboard, do gymnastics, play football, or do any other exercise that puts weight on your bones, they will grow stronger.

Exercise strengthens your muscles and bones.

Stretching is an important part of exercise!

Marvelous muscles

Like bones, muscles need to be used. This doesn't mean you have to go to the gym every day—but if you do not make your muscles work, they become smaller and less fit. Always warm up before working your muscles to prevent tears and strains. Start with slow, gentle movements to warn them that harder exercise is coming. Remember to cool down after exercising too—this helps to prevent muscle damage.

STRANGE BUT TRUE!

It's worth looking after your bones and muscles: they might have to last you a long time. One of the world's oldest people was Jeanne Calment of France, who lived to be 122 years, 164 days old.

Calment was said to have been in perfect health for most of her life. She even took up fencing when she was 85. Calment only began to feel old when she broke her leg—at the age of 114.

Jeanne Calment

BONE AND MUSCLE WORDS

Note: Some boldfaced words are defined where they appear in the book.

cardiac muscle Muscle tissue around the heart

central nervous system The brain and spinal cord

compact bone The hard, dense substance that makes up the outer shell of a bone

contortionist A person who is able to bend his or her body into extreme, unusual shapes

contract To become shorter and tighter

flexible Bendable, or able to move in a lot of different ways

fragile Easily broken

fused Permanently joined together

joint A connection between one bone and another

ligament A fiber that supports the joints of bones, holding them in position

pelvis The bony structure that supports the spine, and has the legs attached to it (at the hips)

plaster cast A hard, light, tube-like case that is built around an arm or leg with a broken bone to protect the bone while it heals

prosthetic Having to do with an artificial body part. An artificial leg, for example, is also called a prosthetic leg.

reflex An automatic response that happens without you thinking about it

scan An image showing what is going on inside someone's body

skeletal muscle A muscle used for movement, which can be voluntarily controlled

smooth muscle Muscle tissue that makes up involuntary muscles, such as those in your digestive system

spinal cord The thick bundle of nerves that carries messages from your brain to the rest of your body and controls body movements

spur Something that sticks out from the main part of an object, such as the three bony knobs that stick out from each vertebra

sternum A long, flat plate of bone in the centre of your chest, to which some of your ribs are attached

tendon The end of a muscle that connects the muscle to a bone

vertebra A bone in the spine, or backbone. The plural of vertebra is vertebrae.

vital Describes something that is essential

FOOD FOR BONES AND MUSCLES

Are you hungry for extra information about bones and muscles? Here are some good places to find out more:

BOOKS TO READ

Burnstein, John. *The Mighty Muscular and Skeletal Systems: How do my bones and muscles work?* Crabtree Publishing, 2009.

Rooney, Anne. *A Math Journey Through the Human Body.* Crabtree Publishing, 2015.

Roza, Greg. *The Muscular System.* Gareth Stevens, 2012.

Roza, Greg. *The Skeletal System.* Gareth Stevens, 2012.

WEBSITES

http://kidshealth.org/kid/htbw/bones.html
http://kidshealth.org/kid/htbw/muscles.html

This website is a really good place to find out all sorts of information about the human body. It has excellent sections on muscles and bones.

www.neok12.com/Skeletal-System.htm

This website has all sorts of information for kids on how the sketelal and muscular systems work, including diagrams, videos, and quizzes.

PLACES TO VISIT

In Boston, Massachusetts, the **Hall of Human Life at the Museum of Science** has over 70 interactive exhibits about how the body works. The museum is located at:

Museum of Science
1 Science Park
Boston, MA 02114
www.mos.org

The **Museum of Science and Industry** in Chicago, Illinois, features YOU! The Experience, a permanent exhibition celebrating human life.
The museum is located at:

The Museum of Science and Industry
5700 S. Lake Shore Drive
Chicago, IL 60637
www.msichicago.org

In Columbus, Ohio, the **Center of Science and Industry** explores the human body in their exhibition Life: The Story of You. The museum is located at:

Center for Science and Industry
333 W. Broad Street
Columbus, OH 43215
www.cosi.org

INDEX